Date: 1/19/16

J 597.878 MAR
Markovics, Joyce L.
My eyes are big and red /

ZOO CLUES

My Eyes Are Big and Red

by Joyce Markovics

Consultants:
Christopher Kuhar, PhD
Executive Director
Cleveland Metroparks Zoo
Cleveland, Ohio

Kimberly Brenneman, PhD
National Institute for Early Education Research
Rutgers University
New Brunswick, New Jersey

BEARPORT PUBLISHING

New York, New York

Credits

Cover, © Juniors Bildarchiv GmbH/Alamy; 4–5, © Aleksey Stemmer/Shutterstock;
6–7, © age fotostock/Alamy; 8–9, © Stephen Dalton/ naturepl.com; 10–11,
© Dirk Ercken/Dreamstime.com; 12–13, © iStockphoto/Thinkstock; 14–15, © Joe
McDonald/Corbis; 16–17, © iStockphoto/Thinkstock; 18–19, © Michael Durham/
Minden Pictures/NGS Image Collection; 20–21, © Michael Durham/Minden
Pictures/NGS Image Collection; 22, © iStockphoto/Thinkstock; 23, © iStockphoto/
Thinkstock; 24, © iStockphoto/Thinkstock.

Publisher: Kenn Goin
Senior Editor: Joyce Tavolacci
Creative Director: Spencer Brinker
Design: Debrah Kaiser
Photo Researcher: Michael Win

Library of Congress Cataloging-in-Publication Data

Markovics, Joyce L.
  My eyes are big and red / by Joyce Markovics ; consultant: Christopher Kuhar, PhD,
Executive Director Cleveland Metroparks Zoo, Cleveland, Ohio.
      pages cm. — (Zoo clues)
  Includes bibliographical references and index.
  ISBN-13: 978-1-62724-110-6 (library binding)
  ISBN-10: 1-62724-110-8 (library binding)
  1. Hylidae—Juvenile literature. I. Title.
  QL668.E24M29 2014
  597.8'78—dc23

                      2013035383

For more information, write to Bearport Publishing Company, Inc., 45 West 21st Street, Suite 3B,
New York, New York 10010. Printed in the United States of America.

10 9 8 7 6 5 4 3 2 1

Contents

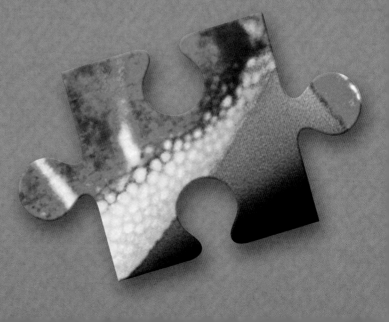

What Am I?

Look at my
feet and toes.

They are orange.

My back is smooth and green.

I have a sticky
pink tongue.

9

My back legs are
long and strong.

11

My nostrils
are tiny.

The sides of my body
are blue and yellow.

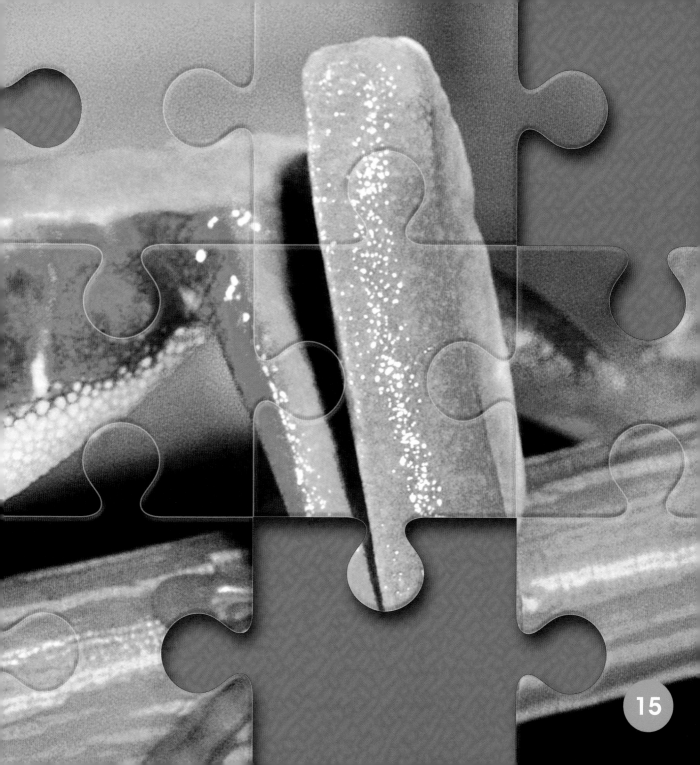

My eyes are
big and red.

What am I?

Let's find out!

I am a red-eyed
tree frog!

20

Animal Facts

Red-eyed tree frogs
are amphibians. Like most
amphibians, they start their
lives in water. Then they
move to dry land when they
grow up.

More Red-eyed Tree Frog Facts

Food:	Crickets, moths, flies, and other insects
Size:	1.5 to 3 inches (3.8 to 7.6 cm) long
Weight:	0.2 to 0.5 ounces (5.6 to 14 g)
Life Span:	5 to 8 years
Cool Fact:	Red-eyed tree frogs have sticky pads on their toes. The pads help them climb and hold onto wet leaves.

Adult Red-eyed
Tree Frog Size

Where Do I Live?

Red-eyed tree frogs live in rain forests in Central and South America.

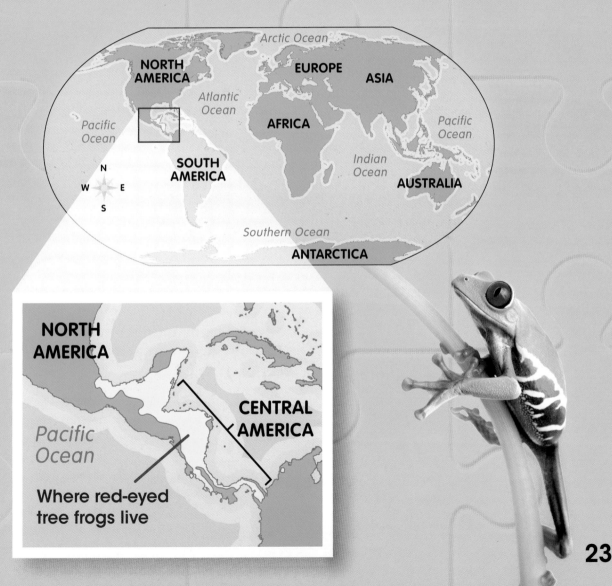

Arctic Ocean

NORTH
AMERICA

EUROPE

ASIA

Atlantic
Ocean

Pacific
Ocean

AFRICA

Pacific
Ocean

N

Indian
Ocean

W
E

SOUTH
AMERICA

S

AUSTRALIA

Southern Ocean

ANTARCTICA

NORTH
AMERICA

CENTRAL
AMERICA

Pacific
Ocean

Where red-eyed
tree frogs live

Index

Read More

Cowley, Joy. *Red-Eyed Tree Frog.* New York: Scholastic (2006).

Phillips, Dee. *Tree Frog (Treed: Animal Life in the Trees).* New York: Bearport (2014).

Learn More Online

To learn more about red-eyed tree frogs, visit
www.bearportpublishing.com/ZooClues

About the Author

Joyce Markovics lives along the Hudson River in Tarrytown, New York. She enjoys spending time with furry, finned, and feathered creatures.